World Languages

Families in
English

Daniel Nunn

Chicago, Illinois

To contact Capstone Global Library please phone 800-747-4992, or visit our website www.capstonepub.com

Edited by Daniel Nunn, Rebecca Rissman & Sian Smith
Designed by Joanna Hinton-Malivoire
Picture research by Tracy Cummins
Production by Victoria Fitzgerald
Originated by Capstone Global Library Ltd
Printed and bound in China by Leo Paper Products Ltd

16 15 14 13 12
10 9 8 7 6 5 4 3 2 1

Library of Congress Cataloging-in-Publication Data
Nunn, Daniel.
  Families in English / Daniel Nunn.
     p. cm.—(World languages - Families)
  Includes bibliographical references and index.
  ISBN 978-1-4329-7177-9—ISBN 978-1-4329-7184-7 (pbk.) 1. English language—Textbooks for foreign speakers—Juvenile literature. 2. Families—Juvenile literature. I. Title.

PE1128.N87 2013
428.1—dc23   2012020434

Acknowledgments
We would like to thank the following for permission to reproduce photographs: Shutterstock pp.4 (Catalin Petolea), 5 (optimarc), 5, 6, 23 (Petrenko Andriy), 5, 7, 22 (Tyler Olson), 5, 8, 23 (Andrey Shadrin), 9, 22 (Erika Cross), 10 (Alena Brozova), 5, 11 (Maxim Petrichuk), 12 (auremar), 13 (Mika Heittola), 5, 14, 15, 22 (Alexander Raths), 5, 16 (Samuel Borges), 17, 23 (Vitalii Nesterchuk), 18 (pat138241), 19 (Fotokostic), 20 (Cheryl Casey), 21 (spotmatik).

Cover photographs of two women and a man reproduced with permission of Shutterstock (Yuri Arcurs). Cover photograph of a girl reproduced with permission of istockphoto (© Sean Lockes). Back cover photograph of a girl reproduced with permission of Shutterstock (Erika Cross).

Every effort has been made to contact copyright holders of any material reproduced in this book. Any omissions will be rectified in subsequent printings if notice is given to the publisher.

Contents

Hello!

My name is Daniel.

And this is my family.

My Mother and Father

my mother

This is my mother.

This is my father.

My Brother and Sister

my brother

This is my brother.

This is my sister.

My Stepmother
and Stepfather

my stepmother

This is my stepmother.

my stepfather

This is my stepfather.

My Stepbrother and Stepsister

my stepbrother

This is my stepbrother.

my stepsister

This is my stepsister.

My Grandmother and Grandfather

my grandmother

This is my grandmother.

my grandfather

This is my grandfather.

My Aunt and Uncle

my aunt

This is my aunt.

my uncle

This is my uncle.

My Cousins

my cousin

These are my cousins.

my cousin

My Friends

my friend

These are my friends.

my friend

21

Can You Remember?

1. Is this my mother or my grandmother?

2. Is this my uncle or my father?

3. Is this my sister or my friend?

4. Is this my stepfather or my uncle?

5. Is this my brother or my cousin?

6. Is this my mother or my aunt?

Answers on page 24

Index

Answers to questions on pages 22 and 23
1. This is my grandmother.
2. This is my father.
3. This is my sister.
4. This is my uncle.
5. This is my brother.
6. This is my mother.